THE
FAIR
DEBT
COLLECTION
PRACTICES
ACT

Fast Read Books
July 2011

Greensboro, NC
Fort Worth,   TX

Self Help Book

Table of Contents

§ 801. Short Title

This title may be cited as the "Fair Debt Collection Practices Act."

§ 802. Congressional findings and declaration of purpose

(a) There is abundant evidence of the use of abusive, deceptive, and unfair debt
collection practices by many debt collectors. Abusive debt collection practices
contribute to the number of personal bankruptcies, to marital instability, to the
loss of jobs, and to invasions of individual privacy.

(b) Existing laws and procedures for redressing these injuries are inadequate to
protect consumers.

(c) Means other than misrepresentation or other abusive debt collection practices are
available for the effective collection of debts.

(d) Abusive debt collection practices are carried on to a substantial extent in interstate

commerce and through means and instrumentalities of such commerce. Even
where abusive debt collection practices are purely intrastate in character, they
nevertheless directly affect interstate commerce.

(e) It is the purpose of this title to eliminate abusive debt collection practices by debt
collectors, to insure that those debt collectors who refrain from using abusive
debt collection practices are not competitively disadvantaged, and to promote
consistent State action to protect consumers against debt collection abuses.

§ 803. Definitions

As used in this title—

(1) The term "Commission" means the Federal Trade Commission.

(2) The term "communication" means the conveying of information regarding a
debt directly or indirectly to any person through any medium.

(3) The term "consumer" means any natural person obligated or allegedly obligated to pay any debt.

(4) The term "creditor" means any person who offers or extends credit creating a debt or to whom a debt is owed, but such term does not include
any person to the extent that he receives an assignment or transfer of a
debt in default solely for the purpose of facilitating collection of such debt for another.
(5) The term "debt" means any obligation or alleged obligation of a consumer to
pay money arising out of a transaction in which the money, property,
insurance or services which are the subject of the transaction are primarily for
personal, family, or household purposes, whether or not such obligation has
been reduced to judgment.
(6) The term "debt collector" means any person who uses any instrumentality of
interstate commerce or the mails in any business the principal purpose of which is the collection of any debts, or who regularly collects or attempts to

collect, directly or indirectly, debts owed or due or asserted to be owed or due another. Notwithstanding the exclusion provided by clause (F) of the last sentence of this paragraph, the term includes any creditor who, in the process of collecting his own debts, uses any name other than his own which would indicate that a third person is collecting or attempting to collect such debts.

For the purpose of section 808(6), such term also includes any person who uses any instrumentality of interstate commerce or the mails in any business the principal purpose of which is the enforcement of security interests. The term does not include—

(A) any officer or employee of a creditor while, in the name of the creditor, collecting debts for such creditor;

(B) any person while acting as a debt collector for another person, both of whom are related by common ownership or affiliated by corporate control, if the person acting as a debt collector does so only 4 § 803 15 USC

1692a for persons to whom it is so related or affiliated and if the principal business of such person is not the collection of debts;

(C) any officer or employee of the United States or any State to the extent that collecting or attempting to collect any debt is in the performance of his official duties;

(D) any person while serving or attempting to serve legal process on any other person in connection with the judicial enforcement of any debt;

(E) any nonprofit organization which, at the request of consumers, performs bona fide consumer credit counseling and assists consumers in the liquidation of their debts by receiving payments from such consumers and distributing such amounts to creditors; and

(F) any person collecting or attempting to collect any debt owed or due or asserted to be owed or due another to the extent such activity

(i) is incidental to a bona fide fiduciary obligation or a bona fide escrow arrangement;

(ii) concerns a debt which was originated by such person;

(iii) concerns a debt which was not in default at the time it was obtained by such person; or

(iv) concerns a debt obtained by such person as a secured party in a commercial credit transaction involving the creditor.

(7) The term "location information" means a consumer's place of abode and his
telephone number at such place, or his place of employment.

(8) The term "State" means any State, territory, or possession of the United States,
the District of Columbia, the Commonwealth of Puerto Rico, or any political
subdivision of any of the foregoing.5 § 804 15 USC 1692b

§ 804. Acquisition of location information

Any debt collector communicating with any person other than
the consumer for the purpose of acquiring location information
about the consumer shall—

(1) identify himself, state that he is confirming or correcting
location information concerning the consumer, and, only

if expressly requested, identify his employer;

(2) not state that such consumer owes any debt;

(3) not communicate with any such person more than once unless requested to do so by such person or unless the debt collector reasonably believes that the earlier response of such person is erroneous or incomplete and that such person now has correct or complete location information;

(4) not communicate by post card;

(5) not use any language or symbol on any envelope or in the contents of any communication effected by the mails or telegram that indicates that the debt collector is in the debt collection business or that the communication relates to the collection of a debt; and

(6) after the debt collector knows the consumer is represented by an attorney with regard to the subject debt and has knowledge of, or can readily ascertain, such attorney's name and address, not communicate with any person

other than that attorney, unless the attorney fails to
respond within a reasonable period of time to the
communication from the debt collector.

§ 805. Communication in connection with debt collection

(a) COMMUNICATION WITH THE CONSUMER GENERALLY.
Without the prior consent of the consumer given
directly to the debt collector or the express permission of a
court of competent jurisdiction, a debt collector may not
communicate with a consumer in connection with the collection
of any debt—
(1) at any unusual time or place or a time or place known or
which should be known to be inconvenient to the

15 USC 1692b

15 USC 1692c6 § 805 15 USC 1692c

consumer. In the absence of knowledge of
circumstances to the contrary, a debt collector
shall assume that the convenient time for

communicating with a consumer is after 8
o'clock antimeridian and before 9 o'clock
postmeridian, local time at the consumer's
location;
(2) if the debt collector knows the consumer is
represented by an attorney with respect to
such debt and has knowledge of, or can
readily ascertain, such attorney's name and
address, unless the attorney fails to respond
within a reasonable period of time to a
communication from the debt collector or
unless the attorney consents to direct
communication with the consumer; or
(3) at the consumer's place of employment if the
debt collector knows or has reason to know
that the consumer's employer prohibits the
consumer from receiving such communication.
(b) COMMUNICATION WITH THIRD PARTIES.

Except as provided in section 804, without the
prior consent of the consumer given directly to the
debt collector, or the express permission of a court
of competent jurisdiction, or as reasonably
necessary to effectuate a postjudgment judicial
remedy, a debt collector may not communicate, in
connection with the collection of any debt, with
any person other than a consumer, his attorney, a
consumer reporting agency if otherwise permitted
by law, the creditor, the attorney of the creditor, or
the attorney of the debt collector.
(c) CEASING COMMUNICATION. If a consumer
notifies a debt collector in writing that the
consumer refuses to pay a debt or that the
consumer wishes the debt collector to cease
further communication with the consumer, the

debt collector shall not communicate further with
the consumer with respect to such debt, except—
(1) to advise the consumer that the debt collector's
further efforts are being terminated;
(2) to notify the consumer that the debt collector or
creditor may invoke specified remedies which
are ordinarily invoked by such debt collector
or creditor; or 7 § 805 15 USC 1692c
(3) where applicable, to notify the consumer that
the debt collector or creditor intends to invoke
a specified remedy.
If such notice from the consumer is made by mail,
notification shall be complete upon receipt.
(d) For the purpose of this section, the term
"consumer" includes the consumer's spouse,
parent (if the consumer is a minor), guardian,
executor, or administrator.

§ 806. Harassment or abuse

A debt collector may not engage in any conduct
the natural consequence of which is to harass, oppress,
or abuse any person in connection with the collection
of a debt. Without limiting the general application of
the foregoing, the following conduct is a violation of
this section:
(1) The use or threat of use of violence or other
criminal means to harm the physical person,
reputation, or property of any person.
(2) The use of obscene or profane language or
language the natural consequence of which is
to abuse the hearer or reader.
(3) The publication of a list of consumers who
allegedly refuse to pay debts, except to a
consumer reporting agency or to persons
meeting the requirements of section 603(f) or
604(3), of this Act.
(4) The advertisement for sale of any debt to coerce

payment of the debt.

(5) Causing a telephone to ring or engaging any

person in telephone conversation repeatedly or

continuously with intent to annoy, abuse, or

harass any person at the called number.

(6) Except as provided in section 804, the

placement of telephone calls without meaningful disclosure of the caller's identity.

1. Section 604(3) has been renumbered as Section 604(a)(3).

15 USC 1692d8 § 807 15 USC 1692e

§ 807. False or misleading representations

A debt collector may not use any false, deceptive,

or misleading representation or means in connection

with the collection of any debt. Without limiting the

general application of the foregoing, the following

conduct is a violation of this section:

(1) The false representation or implication that the

debt collector is vouched for, bonded by, or

affiliated with the United States or any State,
including the use of any badge, uniform, or
facsimile thereof.

(2) The false representation of—

(A) the character, amount, or legal status of
any debt; or

(B) any services rendered or compensation
which may be lawfully received by any debt collector for the collection of a debt.

(3) The false representation or implication that any
individual is an attorney or that any communication is from an attorney.

(4) The representation or implication that
nonpayment of any debt will result in the
arrest or imprisonment of any person or the
seizure, garnishment, attachment, or sale of
any property or wages of any person unless
such action is lawful and the debt collector or
creditor intends to take such action.

(5) The threat to take any action that cannot legally
be taken or that is not intended to be taken.
(6) The false representation or implication that a
sale, referral, or other transfer of any interest
in a debt shall cause the consumer to—
(A) lose any claim or defense to payment of
the debt; or
(B) become subject to any practice prohibited
by this title.
(7) The false representation or implication that the
consumer committed any crime or other
conduct in order to disgrace the consumer.
15 USC 1692e9 § 807 15 USC 1692e
(8) Communicating or threatening to communicate to any person credit information
which is known or which should be known to be
false, including the failure to communicate that a
disputed debt is disputed.

(9) The use or distribution of any written
communication which simulates or is falsely
represented to be a document authorized,
issued, or approved by any court, official, or
agency of the United States or any State, or
which creates a false impression as to its
source, authorization, or approval.
(10) The use of any false representation or
deceptive means to collect or attempt to
collect any debt or to obtain information
concerning a consumer.
(11) The failure to disclose in the initial written
communication with the consumer and, in
addition, if the initial communication with the
consumer is oral, in that initial oral
communication, that the debt collector is
attempting to collect a debt and that any

information obtained will be used for that
purpose, and the failure to disclose in subsequent communications that the communication is from a debt collector,
except that this paragraph shall not apply to a
formal pleading made in connection with a
legal action.

(12) The false representation or implication that
accounts have been turned over to innocent
purchasers for value.

(13) The false representation or implication that
documents are legal process.

(14) The use of any business, company, or
organization name other than the true name of
the debt collector's business, company, or
organization.

(15) The false representation or implication that
documents are not legal process forms or do
not require action by the consumer.

(16) The false representation or implication
that a debt collector operates or is employed by a consumer reporting agency as defined by section 603(f) of
this Act.10 § 808 15 USC 1692f

§ 808. Unfair practices

A debt collector may not use unfair or unconscionable means to collect or attempt to collect
any debt. Without limiting the general application of
the foregoing, the following conduct is a violation of
this section:

(1) The collection of any amount (including any
interest, fee, charge, or expense incidental to
the principal obligation) unless such amount is
expressly authorized by the agreement
creating the debt or permitted by law.

(2) The acceptance by a debt collector from any
person of a check or other payment instrument
postdated by more than five days unless such
person is notified in writing of the debt

collector's intent to deposit such check or

instrument not more than ten nor less than

three business days prior to such deposit.

(3) The solicitation by a debt collector of any

postdated check or other postdated payment

instrument for the purpose of threatening or

instituting criminal prosecution.

(4) Depositing or threatening to deposit any

postdated check or other postdated payment

instrument prior to the date on such check or

instrument.

(5) Causing charges to be made to any person for

communications by concealment of the true

propose of the communication. Such charges

include, but are not limited to, collect telephone calls and telegram fees.

(6) Taking or threatening to take any nonjudicial

action to effect dispossession or disablement

of property if—

(A) there is no present right to possession of

the property claimed as collateral through

an enforceable security interest;

(B) there is no present intention to take

possession of the property; or

(C) the property is exempt by law from such

dispossession or disablement.

15 USC 1692f11 § 808 15 USC 1692f

(7) Communicating with a consumer regarding a

debt by post card.

(8) Using any language or symbol, other than the

debt collector's address, on any envelope

when communicating with a consumer by use

of the mails or by telegram, except that a debt

collector may use his business name if such

name does not indicate that he is in the debt

collection business.

§ 809. Validation of debts

(a) Within five days after the initial communication

with a consumer in connection with the collection
of any debt, a debt collector shall, unless the
following information is contained in the initial
communication or the consumer has paid the debt,
send the consumer a written notice containing—
(1) the amount of the debt;
(2) the name of the creditor to whom the debt is
owed;
(3) a statement that unless the consumer, within
thirty days after receipt of the notice, disputes
the validity of the debt, or any portion thereof,
the debt will be assumed to be valid by the
debt collector;
(4) a statement that if the consumer notifies the debt
collector in writing within the thirty-day period that the debt, or any portion thereof, is
disputed, the debt collector will obtain verification of the debt or a copy of a judgment against the consumer and a copy of

such verification or judgment will be mailed
to the consumer by the debt collector; and
(5) a statement that, upon the consumer's written
request within the thirty-day period, the debt
collector will provide the consumer with the
name and address of the original creditor, if
different from the current creditor.
(b) If the consumer notifies the debt collector in
writing within the thirty-day period described in
subsection (a) that the debt, or any portion thereof,
is disputed, or that the consumer requests the
name and address of the original credi
15 USC 1692g 12 § 809 15 USC 1692g
the debt collector shall cease collection of the
debt, or any disputed portion thereof, until the
debt collector obtains verification of the debt or
any copy of a judgment, or the name and

address of the original creditor, and a copy of
such verification or judgment, or name and
address of the original creditor, is mailed to the
consumer by the debt collector. Collection
activities and communications that do not
otherwise violate this title may continue during
the 30-day period referred to in subsection (a)
unless the consumer has notified the debt
collector in writing that the debt, or any portion of
the debt, is disputed or that the consumer
requests the name and address of the original
creditor. Any collection activities and communication during the 30-day period may not
overshadow or be inconsistent with the
disclosure of the consumer's right to dispute the
debt or request the name and address of the
original creditor.

(c) The failure of a consumer to dispute the validity of a debt under this section may not be construed by any court as an admission of liability by the consumer.

(d) A communication in the form of a formal pleading in a civil action shall not be treated as an initial communication for purposes of subsection (a).

(e) The sending or delivery of any form or notice which does not relate to the collection of a debt and is expressly required by the Internal Revenue Code of 1986, title V of Gramm-Leach-Bliley Act, or any provision of Federal or State law relating to notice of data security breach or privacy, or any regulation prescribed under any such provision of law, shall not be treated as an initial communication in connection with debt collection for purposes of this section.

§ 810. Multiple debts

If any consumer owes multiple debts and makes
any single payment to any debt collector with respect
to such debts, such debt collector may not apply such
payment to any debt which is disputed by the
consumer and, where applicable, shall apply such
payment in accordance with the consumer's
directions.

15 USC 1692h 13 § 811 15 USC 1692i

§ 811. Legal actions by debt collectors

(a) Any debt collector who brings any legal action on
a debt against any consumer shall—
(1) in the case of an action to enforce an interest in
real property securing the consumer's obligation, bring such action only in a judicial
district or similar legal entity in which such
real property is located; or
(2) in the case of an action not described in
paragraph (1), bring such action only in the

judicial district or similar legal entity—
(A) in which such consumer signed the contract sued upon; or
(B) in which such consumer resides at the
commencement of the action.
(b) Nothing in this title shall be construed to authorize
the bringing of legal actions by debt collectors.

§ 812. Furnishing certain deceptive forms

(a) It is unlawful to design, compile, and furnish any
form knowing that such form would be used to
create the false belief in a consumer that a person
other than the creditor of such consumer is
participating in the collection of or in an attempt
to collect a debt such consumer allegedly owes
such creditor, when in fact such person is not so
participating.
(b) Any person who violates this section shall be
liable to the same extent and in the same manner

as a debt collector is liable under section 813 for
failure to comply with a provision of this title.

§ 813. Civil liability

(a) Except as otherwise provided by this section, any
debt collector who fails to comply with any
provision of this title with respect to any person is
liable to such person in an amount equal to the
sum of—

15 USC 1692i
15 USC 1692j

15 USC 1692k14 § 813 15 USC 1692k

(1) any actual damage sustained by such person
as a result of such failure;

(2) (A) in the case of any action by an individual,
such additional damages as the court may
allow, but not exceeding $1,000; or
(B) in the case of a class action,
(i) such amount for each named plaintiff
as could be recovered under subparagraph (A), and
(ii) such amount as the court may allow
for all other class members, without

regard to a minimum individual recovery, not to exceed the lesser of $500,000 or 1 per centum of the net worth of the debt collector; and
(3) in the case of any successful action to enforce the foregoing liability, the costs of the action, together with a reasonable attorney's fee as determined by the court. On a finding by the court that an action under this section was brought in bad faith and for the purpose of harassment, the court may award to the defendant attorney's fees reasonable in relation to the work expended and costs.
(b) In determining the amount of liability in any action under subsection (a), the court shall consider, among other relevant factors—
(1) in any individual action under subsection (a)(2)(A), the frequency and persistence of

noncompliance by the debt collector, the
nature of such noncompliance, and the extent
to which such noncompliance was intentional;
or
(2) in any class action under subsection
(a)(2)(B), the frequency and persistence
of noncompliance by the debt collector,
the nature of such noncompliance, the
resources of the debt collector, the number of persons adversely affected,
and the extent to which the debt collector's noncompliance was intentional. 15 § 813 15 USC 1692k
(c) A debt collector may not be held liable in
any action brought under this title if the
debt collector shows by a preponderance of evidence that the violation was not intentional and resulted from a bona fide error notwithstanding the maintenance of

procedures reasonably adapted to avoid
any such error.
(d) An action to enforce any liability created by this
title may be brought in any appropriate United
States district court without regard to the amount
in controversy, or in any other court of competent
jurisdiction, within one year from the date on
which the violation occurs.
(e) No provision of this section imposing any liability
shall apply to any act done or omitted in good
faith in conformity with any advisory opinion of
the Commission, notwithstanding that after such
act or omission has occurred, such opinion is
amended, rescinded, or determined by judicial or
other authority to be invalid for any reason.

§ 814. Administrative enforcement

(a) Compliance with this title shall be enforced by the

Commission, except to the extent that enforcement of the requirements imposed under
this title is specifically committed to another
agency under subsection (b). For purpose of the
exercise by the Commission of its functions and
powers under the Federal Trade Commission Act,
a violation of this title shall be deemed an unfair
or deceptive act or practice in violation of that
Act. All of the functions and powers of the
Commission under the Federal Trade Commission
Act are available to the Commission to enforce
compliance by any person with this title,
irrespective of whether that person is engaged in
commerce or meets any other jurisdictional tests
in the Federal Trade Commission Act, including
the power to enforce the provisions of this title in

the same manner as if the violation
had been a
violation of a Federal Trade
Commission trade
regulation rule.
(b) Compliance with any requirements
imposed under
this title shall be enforced under—
15 USC 1692/16
(1) section 8 of the Federal Deposit
Insurance
Act, in the case of—
(A) national banks, and Federal
branches and
Federal agencies of foreign banks, by
the
Office of the Comptroller of the
Currency;
(B) member banks of the Federal
Reserve
System (other than national banks),
branches and agencies of foreign
banks
(other than Federal branches, Federal
agencies, and insured State branches
of
foreign banks), commercial lending
companies owned or controlled by
foreign
banks, and organizations operating
under

section 25 or 25(a) of the Federal Reserve
Act, by the Board of Governors of the
Federal Reserve System; and
(C) banks insured by the Federal Deposit
Insurance Corporation (other than
members of the Federal Reserve System)
and insured State branches of foreign
banks, by the Board of Directors of the
Federal Deposit Insurance
Corporation;
(2) section 8 of the Federal Deposit
Insurance Act,
by the Director of the Office of Thrift
Supervision, in the case of a savings
association the deposits of which are
insured
by the Federal Deposit Insurance
Corporation;
(3) the Federal Credit Union Act, by the
Administrator of the National Credit
Union
Administration with respect to any
Federal
credit union;
(4) the Acts to regulate commerce, by
the Secretary
of Transportation, with respect to all
carriers

subject to the jurisdiction of the
Surface
Transportation Board;
(5) the Federal Aviation Act of 1958,
by the
Secretary of Transportation with
respect to
any air carrier or any foreign air carrier
subject
to that Act; and
(6) the Packers and Stockyards Act,
1921 (except as
provided in section 406 of that Act), by
the
Secretary of Agriculture with respect to
any
activities subject to that Act.
§ 814 15 USC 1692/17
The terms used in paragraph (1) that
are not
defined in this title or otherwise
defined in
section 3(s) of the Federal Deposit
Insurance
Act (12 U.S.C. 1813(s)) shall have
the meaning
given to them in section 1(b) of the
International Banking Act of 1978 (12
U.S.C.
3101).
(c) For the purpose of the exercise by
any agency

referred to in subsection (b) of its powers under
any Act referred to in that subsection, a violation
of any requirement imposed under this title shall
be deemed to be a violation of a requirement
imposed under that Act. In addition to its powers
under any provision of law specifically referred to
in subsection (b), each of the agencies referred to
in that subsection may exercise, for the purpose of
enforcing compliance with any requirement
imposed under this title any other authority
conferred on it by law, except as provided in
subsection (d).
(d) Neither the Commission nor any other agency
referred to in subsection (b) may promulgate trade
regulation rules or other regulations with respect
to the collection of debts by debt collectors as
defined in this title.

§ 815. Reports to Congress by the Commission

(a) Not later than one year after the effective date of
this title and at one-year intervals thereafter, the
Commission shall make reports to the Congress
concerning the administration of its functions
under this title, including such recommendations
as the Commission deems necessary or appropriate.
In addition, each report of the Commission shall include its assessment of the
extent to which compliance with this title is being
achieved and a summary of the enforcement
actions taken by the Commission under section
814 of this title.

(b) In the exercise of its functions under this title, the
Commission may obtain upon request the views of
any other Federal agency which exercises

enforcement functions under section 814 of this
title.

15 USC 1692m

§ 814 15 USC 1692/18 § 816 15 USC 1692n

§ 816. Relation to State laws

This title does not annul, alter, or affect, or exempt
any person subject to the provisions of this title from
complying with the laws of any State with respect to
debt collection practices, except to the extent that
those laws are inconsistent with any provision of this
title, and then only to the extent of the inconsistency.
For purposes of this section, a State law is not
inconsistent with this title if the protection such law
affords any consumer is greater than the protection
provided by this title.

§ 817. Exemption for State regulation

The Commission shall by regulation exempt from
the requirements of this title any class of debt

collection practices within any State if the
Commission determines that under the law of that
State that class of debt collection practices is subject
to requirements substantially similar to those imposed
by this title, and that there is adequate provision for
enforcement.

§ 818. Exception for certain bad check enforcement programs operated by private entities

(a) In General.—

(1) TREATMENT OF CERTAIN PRIVATE ENTITIES.—Subject to paragraph (2), a private entity shall be excluded from the definition of a debt collector, pursuant to the exception provided in section 803(6), with respect to the operation by the entity of a program described in paragraph (2)(A) under a contract described in paragraph (2)(B).

(2) CONDITIONS OF APPLICABILITY.—
Paragraph (1) shall apply if—
(A) a State or district attorney establishes,
within the jurisdiction of such State or district attorney and with respect to alleged bad check violations that do not
involve a check described in subsection
(b), a pretrial diversion program for alleged bad check offenders who agree to
participate voluntarily in such program to
avoid criminal prosecution;

15 USC 1692n
15 USC 1692o

15 USC 1692p19 § 818 15 USC 1692p
(B) a private entity, that is subject to an
administrative support services contract with a
State or district attorney and operates under the
direction, supervision, and control of such State
or district attorney, operates the pretrial diversion
program described in subparagraph (A); and
(C) in the course of performing duties

delegated to it by a State or district attorney under the contract, the private entity referred to in subparagraph (B)—

(i) complies with the penal laws of the State;

(ii) conforms with the terms of the contract and directives of the State or district attorney;

(iii) does not exercise independent prosecutorial discretion;

(iv) contacts any alleged offender referred

to in subparagraph (A) for purposes of participating in a program referred to in such paragraph—

(I) only as a result of any determination by the State or district attorney that probable cause of a bad check violation under State penal law exists, and that contact with the alleged offender for purposes of participation in the program is appropriate; and

(II) the alleged offender has failed to pay the bad check after demand for payment, pursuant to State law, is made for payment of the check amount;

(v) includes as part of an initial written communication with an alleged

offender a clear and conspicuous
statement that—
(I) the alleged offender may dispute
the validity of any alleged bad
check violation;
(II) where the alleged offender knows,
or has reasonable cause to
believe, that the alleged bad check
violation is the result of theft or
forgery of the check, identity
theft, 20 § 818 15 USC 1692p or
other fraud that is not the result of
the conduct of the alleged
offender, the alleged offender
may file a crime report with the
appropriate law enforcement
agency; and
(III) if the alleged offender notifies the
private entity or the district
attorney in writing, not later than
30 days after being contacted for
the first time pursuant to clause
(iv), that there is a dispute
pursuant to this subsection, before
further restitution efforts are
pursued, the district attorney or an
employee of the district attorney
authorized to make such a
determination makes a
determination that there is
probable cause to believe that a
crime has been committed; and

(vi) charges only fees in connection with
services under the contract that have
been authorized by the contract with
the State or district attorney.
(b) Certain Checks Excluded.—A check is described
in this subsection if the check involves, or is
subsequently found to involve—
(1) a postdated check presented in connection with
a payday loan, or other similar transaction,
where the payee of the check knew that the
issuer had insufficient funds at the time the
check was made, drawn, or delivered;
(2) a stop payment order where the issuer acted in
good faith and with reasonable cause in
stopping payment on the check;
(3) a check dishonored because of an adjustment to
the issuer's account by the financial institution
holding such account without providing notice
to the person at the time the check
was made,

drawn, or delivered;

(4) a check for partial payment of a debt where the

payee had previously accepted partial payment

for such debt;21 § 818 15 USC 1692p

(5) a check issued by a person who was not

competent, or was not of legal age, to enter

into a legal contractual obligation at the time

the check was made, drawn, or delivered; or

(6) a check issued to pay an obligation arising from

a transaction that was illegal in the jurisdiction

of the State or district attorney at the time the

check was made, drawn, or delivered.

(c) Definitions.—For purposes of this section, the

following definitions shall apply:

(1) STATE OR DISTRICT ATTORNEY.—The

term "State or district attorney" means the

chief elected or appointed prosecuting attorney in a district, county (as defined in

section 2 of title 1, United States Code), municipality,
or comparable jurisdiction,
including State attorneys general who act as
chief elected or appointed prosecuting attorneys in a district, county (as so defined),
municipality or comparable jurisdiction, who
may be referred to by a variety of titles such as
district attorneys, prosecuting attorneys,
commonwealth's attorneys, solicitors, county
attorneys, and state's attorneys, and who are
responsible for the prosecution of State crimes
and violations of jurisdiction-specific local
ordinances.
(2) CHECK.—The term "check" has the same
meaning as in section 3(6) of the Check
Clearing for the 21st Century Act.
(3) BAD CHECK VIOLATION.—The term "bad
check violation" means a violation of the

applicable State criminal law relating to the
writing of dishonored checks.

§ 819. Effective date

This title takes effect upon the expiration of six
months after the date of its enactment, but section 809
shall apply only with respect to debts for which the
initial attempt to collect occurs after such effective
date.

15 USC 1692 note22